BIGFOOT

I0140396

WORLD BOOK

www.worldbook.com

Contents

How to use this book

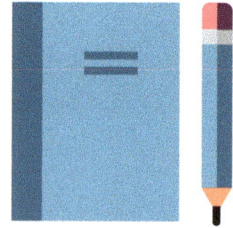

A field guide is a book written to help you identify and learn about animals or other things in nature. The "field" part is just a fancy way of saying you're supposed to carry it with you while tramping about in the wild. A normal field guide will fit in your pocket. This one very probably will not.

A normal field guide is also filled with normal sorts of information about chipmunks and chestnut trees provided by normal experts. This field guide deals with the mysterious Bigfoot, a legendary apelike creature said to roam the woods of North America. Bigfoot "experts" tend to be a mixed bag of amateurs, eccentrics, and outright frauds. You'll just have to deal with it.

The following items may be useful in your search for Bigfoot:

Binoculars

Hiking Boots

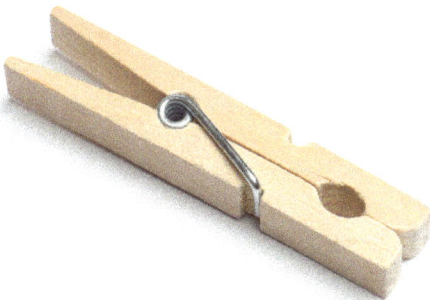

Clothespin
(Put on nose to block the legendary smell.)

Chewbacca Costume
(Sneak up on Bigfoot with this disguise.)

Caution:
If you have ever read a fairy tale, you know that it's dangerous to wander off into the woods in search of legendary monsters. So wear comfortable shoes and be sure to ask a parent's permission.

Description

Thousands of people have reported sightings of Bigfoot. Witnesses describe a humanlike or apelike creature, covered with brown or black hair. Bigfoot walks and stands upright, just like you and I.

One of Bigfoot's most notable features is his giant feet, which lend the elusive creature his name. Bigfoot tracks remain some of the most important "evidence" for the creature's existence.

Size

Bigfoot may look like an ape or a person. But he's probably a bit bigger than anyone you know. Bigfoot is said to stand about 7 to 10 feet (2 to 3 meters) tall. That's taller than your dad, most likely.

Bigfoot is also said to have a thickly built body, weighing between 600 and 1,000 pounds (270 and 450 kilograms). A pair of Bigfoots (or is it Bigfeet?) might weigh as much as a two-seat Smart car.

DAD

BROWN BEAR

BIGFOOT

Anatomy

APELIKE FEATURES

SHAGGY HAIR

STINK LINES

People who have had a close encounter with Bigfoot often report on the beast's distinctive—and unpleasant—body odor.

HUGE FEET

UPRIGHT STANCE

Sasquatch

Many Native American groups tell stories of a Bigfootlike creature called Sasquatch. In fact, some people think Bigfoot and Sasquatch are one and the same. Some Pacific Coast tribes even represent the creature in ceremonial masks and totem poles.

In some Native American traditions, Bigfoot is a peaceful, even helpful creature of the forest. In others, he is feared as a frightening monster.

Dzunukwa is another mythical figure that appears on some totem poles.
She is known as the "Wild Woman of the Woods" and is said to feast on children!

Bigfoot sightings

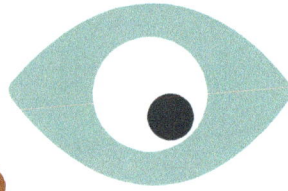

Settlers of the American West have reported encounters with strange, apelike creatures for a long time. In 1924, for example, some gold prospectors reported being attacked by a group of "ape-men" near Mount Saint Helens in Washington state.

In the 1950's, loggers in California reported finding strange large footprints. A series of newspaper articles attributed the prints to a creature named Bigfoot, helping to popularize the name.

Since that time, thousands of people have reported sightings of Bigfoot. In 2019, the FBI even released files showing it had conducted a brief, inconclusive investigation into the matter.

BIG FOOT XING

DUE TO SIGHTINGS IN THE AREA OF A CREATURE RESEMBLING "BIG FOOT" THIS SIGN HAS BEEN POSTED FOR YOUR SAFETY

The New York Times

Is It Bigfoot Or Can It Be Just a Hoax?

Commonly mistaken for Bigfoot

Just because something looks like Bigfoot doesn't mean it is. Here, for comparison, are several things to avoid mistaking for the legendary creature.

BIGFOOT THE MONSTER TRUCK.

Both Bigfoots are large and powerful, but the creature Bigfoot can be distinguished by his lack of wheels.

A BEAR.

Like Bigfoot, the North American brown bear is large, hairy, and lives in the woods.

Commonly mistaken for Bigfoot

(continued)

THE YETI

is the famous *abominable* (dreadful) snowman of the Himalaya mountains. He can be distinguished from Bigfoot by his snowy vibe and abominable manners.

BIGFOOT

YETI

TEDDY BEAR.

If your teddy bear happens to be 10 feet tall, you might mistake it for Bigfoot.

A TALL, HAIRY MAN.

Some dudes are just tall and hairy—perhaps even your dad. That doesn't make him Bigfoot.

THIS YELLOW LINE IS ONLY 13 INCHES.

Tracks

ADD THREE MORE INCHES,

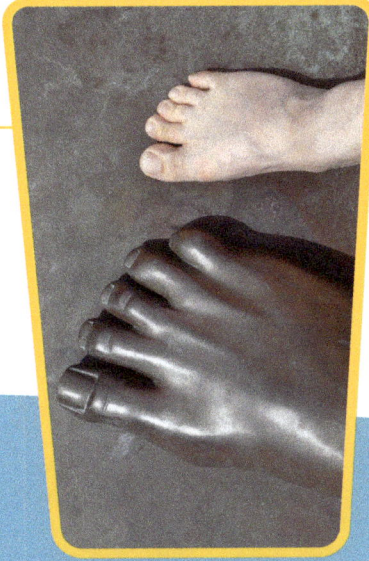

AND YOU HAVE BIGFOOT'S BIG FEET!

Bigfoot "tracks" were some of the first evidence ever presented for the mysterious creature's existence. And as the creature's name suggests, its footprints are real whoppers. Many of them measure about 16 inches (41 centimeters) long and about 7 inches (18 centimeters) wide.

The prints suggest the foot has five toes. It lacks a distinct arch and appears to be more flexible than the human foot.

THE FOOT WON'T EVEN FIT ON THESE TWO PAGES!!!!!!

Hair

Bigfoot hunters have collected small samples of hair from sites where Bigfoot tracks are found. Scientific tests have shown that some of the hair samples come from such shaggy imposters as bear and bison. But other samples have proved difficult to match with any known animal.

Range

Many early sightings of Bigfoot were reported in the mountains of California. Other reports often come from mountainous and wooded areas of Oregon, Washington, and British Columbia.

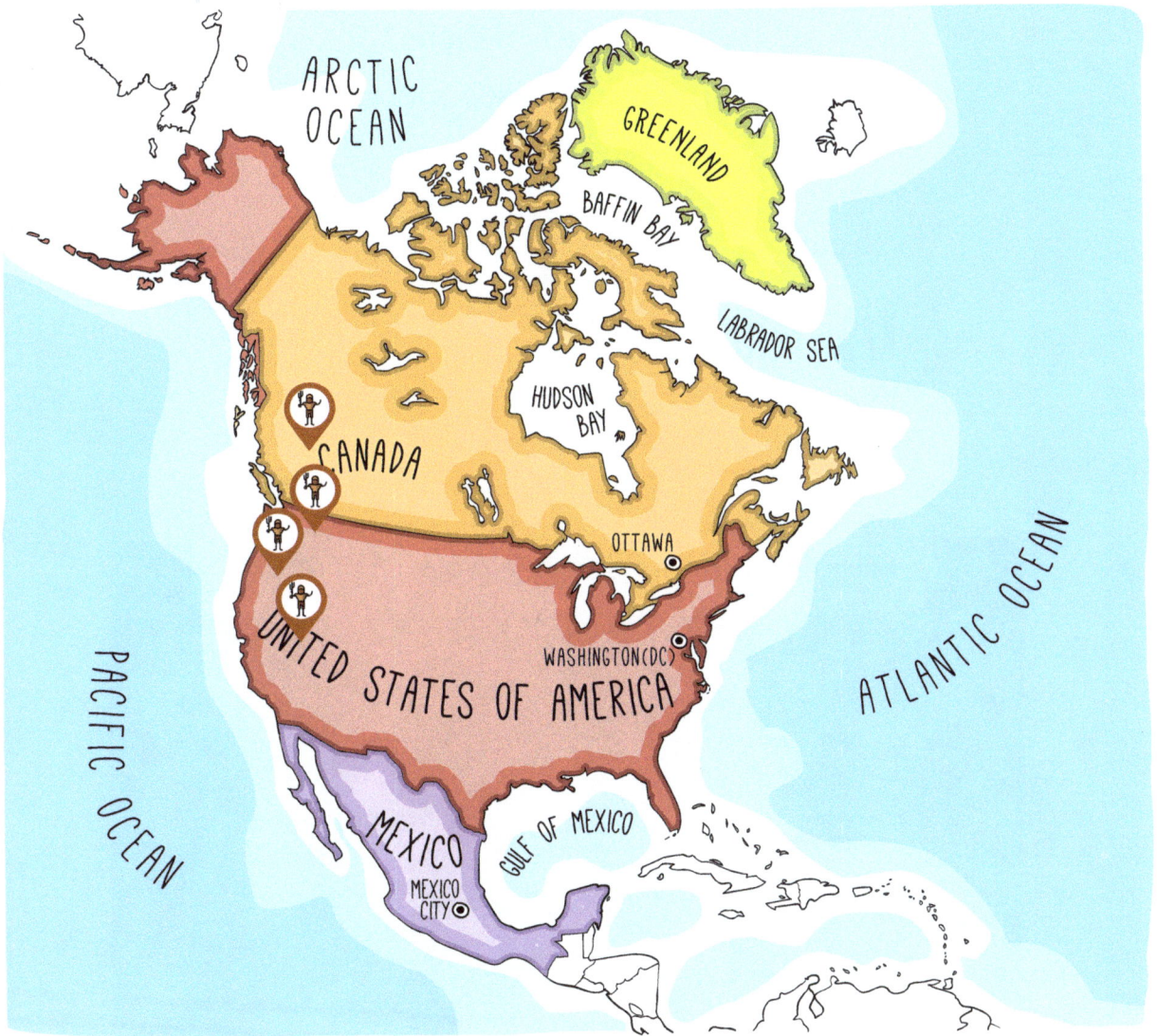

Habitat

Before setting off in search of Bigfoot, it may be helpful to familiarize yourself with various aspects of the creature's habitat.

REDWOOD TREES.

It takes big trees to hide a big monster, and Bigfoot's habitat includes the biggest trees of all. The coast redwood, found in mountainous areas near the U.S. Pacific Coast, typically grows 200 to 300 feet (60 to 90 meters) high, with a trunk 8 to 12 feet (2.4 to 3.7 meters) wide.

GLOOMY WEATHER.

Better pack your umbrella! Moist winds from the Pacific Ocean bring clouds, fog, and rainfall to large portions of Bigfoot's habitat.

Habitat

(continued)

BANANA SLUGS.

Has Bigfoot been dropping bananas all over the forest floor? More likely that's a Pacific banana slug, one of the world's largest slugs. These banana-yellow beauties can grow up to 10 inches (25 centimeters) in length.

HIPSTERS.

The Pacific Northwest is also home to a large population of hipsters. Whilst looking for Bigfoot, you're sure to see plenty of these too-cool youngsters waxing their mustaches, drinking fair-trade coffee, or riding around on fixed-gear bicycles.

Caught on tape

Perhaps the most famous evidence for Bigfoot is a film shot by Roger Patterson and Bob Gimlin in northern California in 1967. The Patterson-Gimlin film is no masterpiece—it's mostly just some grainy footage of the two men horsing around in the woods. (They were literally riding horses.)

But, a few minutes in, an apelike creature strides across the wooded scene, even appearing to glance back at the camera. To some people, the film is the best evidence that Bigfoot exists. To others, it looks like a guy monkeying around in a gorilla suit.

Bigfoot dos and don'ts

DON'T PLAY BASKETBALL WITH BIGFOOT.

Bigfoot is up to 10 feet (3 meters) tall with long, apelike arms. He will dunk on you so hard you will never be able to show your face in public again.

Bigfoot dos and don'ts

(continued)

DO TRY TO DRAW BIGFOOT OUT BY PLAYING GRUNGE MUSIC.

This raw, forceful style of music, made famous by such bands as Nirvana and Soundgarden, developed in the Seattle, Washington, area in the early 1990's. It is likely to make a grown-up Bigfoot nostalgic for his rebellious youth.

Bigfoot dos and don'ts

(continued)

DON'T SHOOT BIGFOOT.

In many eyewitness accounts, Bigfoot appears to be a shy, peaceful creature. He just wants to be left alone, man. What did Bigfoot ever do to you?

Bigfoot around the world

Bigfoot isn't alone—legends of mysterious ape-men abound around the world. Here are just a few local names for Bigfootlike creatures.

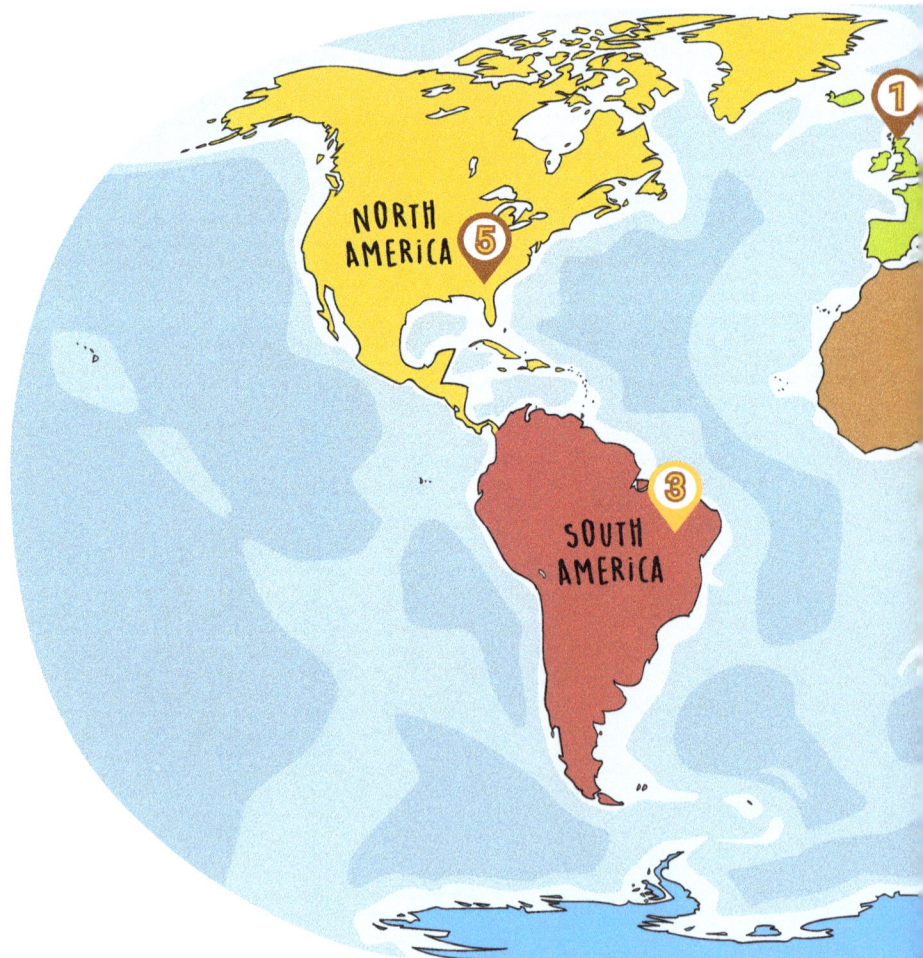

NORTH AMERICA

SOUTH AMERICA

1. Grey Man–Scotland
2. Mande Barung–India
3. Mapinguari–Brazil
4. Orang Pendek–Indonesia
5. Skunk ape–Southeastern United States
6. Yeti–Himalaya
7. Yowie–Australia

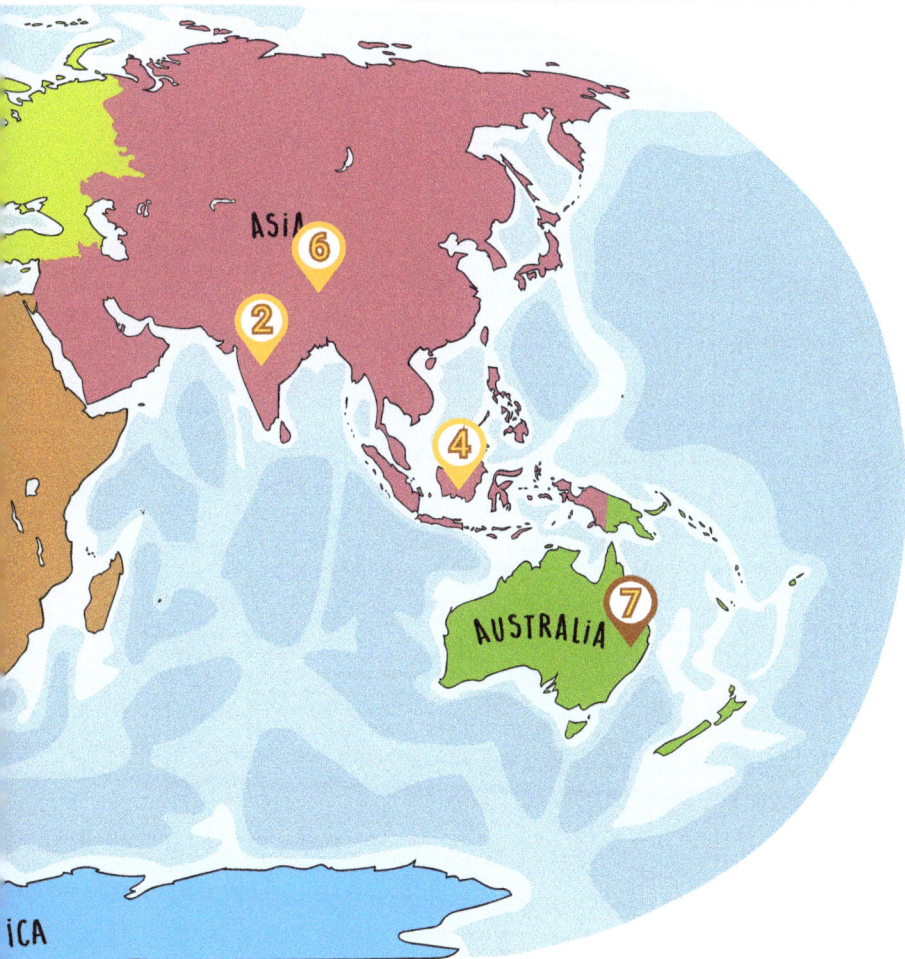

ASIA

AUSTRALIA

ICA

Classification

Without any solid evidence, it's hard to say exactly what Bigfoot is. Many people think the beast may be some undiscovered species related to human beings.

Fossils show, for example, that modern human beings had a lot of big, hairy ancestors. Some people think that Bigfoot could actually be a small population of straggling survivors of such prehistoric people. That makes Bigfoot kind of like your tall, hairy uncle who lives in the woods (the one the rest of your family don't like to talk about).

Classification

(continued)

Some people think the idea of Bigfoot is even older. They think that Bigfoot stories trace back to fossils or memories of long extinct creatures.

One such creature is *Gigantopithecus*, a huge extinct ape that once lived in the forests of what are now southern China, northern Vietnam, and northern India. *Gigantopithecus* lived from about 8 million years ago to about 200,000 years ago.

Some *Gigantopithecus* may have weighed more than 900 pounds (400 kilograms) and stood 10 feet (3 meters) tall when upright. That sounds like Bigfoot to me!

Status

Many scientists and other experts doubt that Bigfoot really exists. They may chalk up various Bigfoot encounters to mistaken identity, tall tales, and outright *hoaxes* (deliberate pranks). No footprints, hair, or other evidence have ever provided clear evidence that Bigfoot is real.

But, scientists are a weird bunch. As much as they love evidence, they also value being open-minded. It may be very, very unlikely that such a large creature has lived undiscovered for hundreds of years, but the woods of North America are a vast and often wild place.

Index

Written by Jeff De La Rosa
Illustrations by Alex Pearson, Familytree

Directed by Tom Evans
Designed by Matt Carrington
Photo edited by Rosalia Bledsoe
Proofread by Nathalie Strassheim
Indexed by David Pofelski
Manufacturing led by Anne Fritzinger

World Book, Inc.
180 North LaSalle Street, Suite 900
Chicago, Illinois 60601
USA

For information about other World Book print and digital publications, please go to

www.worldbook.com or call 1-800-WORLDBK (967-5325).

For information about sales to schools and libraries,
call 1-800-975-3250 (United States) or 1-800-837-5365 (Canada).

Library of Congress Cataloging-in-Publication Data for this volume has been applied for.

Abnormal Field Guides to Cryptic Creatures
ISBN: 978-0-7166-4149-0 (set, hc.)

Bigfoot
ISBN: 978-0-7166-4150-6 (hc.)

Also available as:
ISBN: 978-0-7166-4158-2 (e-book)

1st printing March 2020

WORLD
BOOK
www.worldbook.com

www.ingramcontent.com/pod-product-compliance
Lightning Source LLC
Chambersburg PA
CBHW061411090426

42741CB00021B/3480